The Abolition Plays

Head in the Game and *The Intimacy Coordinator*

By Carolyn Gage

Introduction

Theatre is a tremendously powerful vehicle for social change. Why? Because it takes place in real time with a live audience who actively participate in the collective experience of creating a make-believe world. Theatre does not describe, theorize about, take pictures of, or outline steps for achieving a different reality. It brings that reality to life in real time and real space, and audiences who are present in the room for that hour or two will carry away a *living memory* of that alternative world. And the power of a lived memory cannot be over-estimated.

I recently produced a Zoom reading of two social change plays, *Head in the Game* and *The Intimacy Coordinator*. These are both plays that support the abolition of prostitution, advocating for immediate adoption of the Nordic model. The reading was followed by a talkback with Dr. Melissa Farley, founder and director of the non-profit organization, Prostitution Research and Education. Both plays present models that confront audiences with the contradictions, disconnects, false assumptions, and denials that support the liberal lies that prostitution is a legitimate and even empowering career choice.

Head in the Game

Head in the Game was inspired by an online interview from *RTÉ's Morning Edition* with Rachel Moran, the author of *Paid For: My Journey Through Prostitution*. Moran is a brilliant and eloquent anti-prostitution activist who was prostituted for seven years, from age fifteen to twenty-two. Here is the excerpt that inspired my play:

> *Interviewer: You describe it [prostitution] as a form of sexual abuse. Tell me why.*
>
> *Rachel Moran: Because unwanted sex is unwanted sex...*

Interviewer: Even if you're being paid for it.

Rachel Moran: Oh, yes. Money doesn't have any kind of magical quality that can remove the feelings that you feel in yourself when you're having unwanted sex... and I always make the comparison if I was to hand somebody twenty quid and give them a smack in the mouth, that wouldn't do anything to take the sting out the slap, you know.

Interviewer: And I suppose some people might say, "Well, there is a difference there in that a woman might offer herself for paid sex rather than offer herself for a slap in the mouth." You know... is there another side to that argument at all, in your mind, Rachel?

Rachel Moran: Well, no, because—the funny part about it is receiving violence for money is part of prostitution. There's plenty of men out there who'd pay you to do exactly that.

Moran's analogy is so incontrovertible and so apt, I decided to build a one-act around the conceit of males buying access to women's bodies for the purpose of punching them in what they refer to as a recreational form of "boxing." They women are not allowed to punch back or even defend themselves. These so-called sparring partners, aka "Boxing Girls," are in no way partners, and what is going on is obviously paid abuse.

In the play, a reporter and her intern, both women, are infiltrating a Boxing Girls Gym in order to do a story for *Gentlemen Magazine*. While there, a policeman shows up to investigate a report of a man beating up a woman. When he realizes where he is, however, he stops asking questions, because everyone knows the Boxing Girl Gyms are a licensed franchise for recreational purposes. The victim of the beating finds that the owner of the gym is more concerned about the

iv

interruption of service for the client than the injuries of his victim. The owner sends the policeman off with a stack of Boxing Girl Gym business cards to share down at the station, and then reminds the battered employee that she has rent to pay and a daughter to support. The owner of the francise encourages the young woman to take the proferred painkillers, chill out in the break room, and prepare for her next round of "sparring." The visiting journalist's attempt to protect the victim results in her own arrest for trespassing and assault.

Enlarging on Moran's analogy, the Boxing Girls Gym is obviously a front for abuse. The non-reciprocal nature of the punching is so blatant that everyone can see through the lie of referring to the employees as "sparring partners." Why isn't it as obvious that the interactions in prostitution are just as one-sided and just as abusive—if not more so? If the sexual activity of the john is not welcome, not desired, and not reciprocal, why is it even considered "sex?"

Could it be because, in patriarchy, sex has always been defined by men from their perspective and serving their interests? Is it because sex between so-called intimate partners is so often not mutual or egalitarian? Isn't this evident from the continued use of the word "foreplay" to describe activities that are overwhelmingly the "main events" with regard to women's arousal and orgasm? The myth of the vaginal orgasm still holds sway in a popular culture that routinely misapplies the word "vagina" to refer to the "vulva"—in effect, performing a linguistic clitorectomy. And, of course, for millions of women, clitorectomy is literal. I want my audiences to consider why they characterize prostitution as the selling of "sex" and not paid abuse, when the desire so clearly is not reciprocal.

Once paid abuse is framed as recreational and consensual, the police become complicit. Liberal reformers can only direct their efforts at harm reduction, as if the right to inflict that harm is not the very service being offered.

Head in the Game is an intentionally short play—only fifteen minutes—to allow for forty-five minutes of post-show discussion in a classroom or conference workshop.

The Intimacy Coordinator

The second play, **The Intimacy Coordinator**, builds on this concept of one-sided desire, focusing on the prostituted woman as a performer who is putting on an act—enacting the role of a woman who is as desirous of sex as the john, and specifically desirous of whatever he dictates. In the world of theatre and film today, actors who are given roles that require physical intimacy are entitled to protections against sexual harassment and sexual violation. A whole industry of "intimacy coordinators" has sprung up to choreograph intimate scenes, ensuring that every action and every word will be mutually consensual and that no boundaries will be crossed. The introduction of the intimacy coordinator into a brothel is perceived immediately by the audience as absurd... but why is that? Because the right to non-consensual access *is* the specific commodity that has been purchased. The presence of an intimacy coordinator, reminding everyone that the sexual activity is one-way and actually unwelcome, defeats the whole purpose for the john.

The Intimacy Coordinator raises inescapable questions about prostitution as legitimate work. Why isn't the prostituted woman afforded the same protections as an actress? Why is she not afforded the same protections of health care workers whose jobs expose them to the bio-hazards of sweat, blood, semen, urine, saliva, etc. Worker protections for these employees include latex gloves, gowns, aprons, protective clothing, masks, and eye protection defined as goggles or glasses with side shields or chin-length face shields. Again, this would be considered a ridiculous conceit when applied to prostitution. And again, I ask why. Why should the john's purchase of services override the prostituted woman's entitlement to standard worker protections for performers and health care workers? Because, as *The Intimacy Coordinator* makes clear, it's not and never can be legitimate work, but is *paid abuse*.

Both of these one-acts invite audiences to inhabit alternative worlds that are the logical extensions of their assumptions about prostitution. The contradictions and absurdities of these assumptions are immediate and visceral, the audience now has a memory inside their brain that conflicts with their thinking, and that is the greatest of all agents for social change.

Head in the Game

Dedicated to Rachel Moran

Summary

The play opens outside the Boxing Girls Gym. In the Boxing Girls Gym, clients (nearly all male) pay by the hour to "spar" with the women who work there, the "boxing girls." In this form of "boxing," the boxing girls are not allowed to hit back or defend themselves. The client pays to "win." In the eyes of the law, the activity is recreational and considered just another form of boxing.

In the play, a reporter and her intern, both women, are infiltrating a Boxing Girls Gym in order to do a story for *Gentlemen Magazine*. While they are there, a policeman shows up to investigate a report of a man beating up a woman. When he realizes where he is, he stops asking questions. The victim of the beating runs on, begging for protection. The owner of the gym, showing more concern for the client's interrupted service, sends another "boxing girl" to finish "sparring."

The head of the gym sends the policeman off with a stack of Boxing Girls business cards, and she counsels the victim not to pursue the matter. She reminds the boxing girl that she has a daughter at home she can barely support, offers her drugs, and sends her to the Makeup Room to prepare for another "round."

Meanwhile, the intern has become increasingly upset by what she sees as blatant violence against women. Her attempt to rescue the victim is ends with a nasty twist.

5 women, 20-35
1 male
Single set (first scene can be done on apron)
20 minutes

Cast of Characters

SARAH: Young woman, college student, 20's, interning on the side. Working-class background.

KAI: Young professional, early 30's. Career journalist. Middle-class.

POLICEMAN: Male, any age.

HARLEY: Young woman, same age as KAI. Aggressive, entrepreneurial.

CONNIE: Young woman, 20's. Poor, single mom.

MARISA: Young woman, late teens or early 20's.

Scene

Sidewalk and interior of Boxing Girls Gym.

Time

The present

Head in the Game

Scene 1

Lights come up on the sidewalk outside the entrance to Boxing Girls Gym, a new establishment in an urban area. SARAH and KAI are talking. SARAH is in her mid-to-late 20's. She's a college student from a working-class background, and part-time intern at Gentlemen's Magazine. *KAI, early 30's, works full-time for the magazine. Raised middle-class, she is very much the young professional on her way up.*

SARAH: *(Looking at the sign.)* So this is it...

KAI: Yep. *(Reading.)* "Boxing Girls Gym."

SARAH: Do you think they'll believe us?

KAI: Why wouldn't they?

SARAH: Because I've never been undercover before.

KAI: *(Annoyed.)* We're not "undercover."

SARAH: But you said we weren't going to tell them we're from *Gentlemen Magazine*... that you didn't want them to know we were journalists and that we were going to pretend that we were there because we wanted to be boxing girls.

KAI: First off, only *one* of us is a professional journalist... *(Patronizing smile.)* You're an *intern*—

SARAH: But what if they find out we're spying on them, and they beat us up?

KAI: Why would they do that?

SARAH: Because that's what they do, isn't it? *(KAI look at her.)* The "boxing girls….?" *(Pause.)* Hello…? The men come in and beat them up.

KAI: *(Shaking her head.)* That is *not* what they do at all. The men come in and *pay* to *spar* with the girls. They pay for a sparring partner's *time*. It's a gym. There's a ring. It's *boxing*. That's why they call them "boxing girls."

SARAH: But the boxing girls aren't allowed to punch back or defend themselves—

KAI: *(Exasperated with SARAH's slowness.)* They're paid to let the men win.

SARAH: They're paid to get *beat up.*

KAI: And football players are paid to get concussions. You can look at it that way if you want to, but it's a sport.

SARAH: But in football, the whole point of the game isn't the—

KAI: They get *paid.* They're not victims. It's a job, a career. No, it's not for everyone, but then again… *(Pointedly.)* … neither is journalism.

SARAH: I'm just trying to understand… If it's so legitimate, then why aren't we going to tell them we're from *Gentlemen Magazine*?

KAI: Because most people get nervous talking to journalists. We can get a better view of their operation if they treat us like insiders.

SARAH: My name is going to be "Jean."

KAI: We don't need fake names. They aren't going to know who we are anyway.

SARAH: *(Getting into it.)* I always wanted to be "Jean." I look kind of like a "Jean," don't' I?

KAI: *(Shaking her head.)* I have to file the story tonight. Come on…

SARAH: *(Prompting her.)* "Jean."

KAI: *(Rolling her eyes.)* C'mon, "Jean." *(SARAH beams. They exit into the gym, SARAH doing her "Jean" strut.)*

End of Scene

Scene 2

Lights come up on the lobby of the Boxing Girls Gym. There is a front desk and a row of chairs. MARISA, a nervous young woman in her early 20's or late teens, is sitting in one of the chairs. She wears boxing attire, but otherwise in no way looks athletic. HARLEY, a woman in her 30's, owns the franchise. She stands behind a large counter. She is busy with bookkeeping. Behind her is a row of keys to the different sparring rooms. KAI enters, with SARAH following. KAI steps up to the desk. HARLEY doesn't look up.

KAI: Hello…?

HARLEY: *(Looking up, she checks out KAI and SARAH.)* Yeah?

KAI: We're here to box…

HARLEY: *(Looking down at her books again.)* That's $100 an hour, and I need to have the cash up front.

SARAH: What?

HARLEY: $100 for an hour of sparring. Apiece.

KAI: No… We're not here to *hire* a boxing girl. We want to apply.

SARAH: *(To KAI.)* Wait… You mean *women* come in here to… to—

KAI: *(Cutting her off.)* To box. Of course. Why wouldn't they? Boxing is an equal opportunity sport.

SARAH: I just thought—

KAI: *(To HARLEY.)* Do we have to fill out something…? A job application…?

HARLEY: *(Suspicious.)* Where did you hear about us?

SARAH: *(Quickly.)* At the university. Some of the girls in my dorm were boxing girls over the summer.

HARLEY: *(Eying her.)* You're a student?

SARAH: Yes.

HARLEY: *(Nodding, turning to KAI.)* What about you?

KAI: Oh, single mom. You probably see a lot of us.

HARLEY: Not usually in designer clothes. *(SARAH looks anxiously over at KAI.)*

KAI: I have expensive tastes. Here to support my habit. *(She attempts to stare down HARLEY. HARLEY doesn't respond.)*

SARAH: But *I* really *am* a student. *(KAI gives her the side eye. HARLEY looks at the two of them.)*

HARLEY: Any prior experience?

SARAH: Not boxing, but I took some self-defense classes. *(HARLEY stares at her.)*

KIA: *(To SARAH, between her teeth.)* Relevant to the job.

SARAH: Battered women's shelter…?

HARLEY: *(Exasperated.)* Massage parlor. Escort service. Exotic dancing.

SARAH: Oh… Then I guess not. *(HARLEY turns to KAI.)*

KAI: Waitress at a strip club.

HARLEY: You can both intern. Unpaid. And you gotta sign a waiver.

SARAH: Is that legal?

HARLEY: *(To KAI.)* Take it or leave it.

KAI: We're in. *(HARLEY slides some papers toward her.)*

SARAH: What's the waiver for?

KAI: *(To SARAH, exasperated.)* Oh, for god's sake, Sarah! It's a *gym waiver*—

SARAH: *(Correcting her.)* "Jean."

KAI: Sarah-Jean. You have to sign them for any gym. You have to sign them for yoga classes…

SARAH: *(To HARLEY, with a little swagger.)* My *friends* call me "Jean."

HARLEY: *(Not impressed.)* Well, "Jean," sign here.

SARAH: *(Holding up a finger, she begins to read:)* "I hereby agree to assume all risks attendant upon myself while participating in this gym. As a result of my participation on the Boxing Girls Gym, LLC, I hereby waive, release, and discharge any and all claims for personal injury, or property damage which I may have, or which may hereafter accrue to me, or death… *(She looks up.)* "Death…?" *(Suddenly the door swings open and the POLICEMAN barges in. He turns initially to KAI and SARAH.)*

HARLEY: *(Behind the desk.)* May I help you?

POLICEMAN: *(Turning to HARLEY.)* Police… *(Flashing a badge, he speaks aggressively.)* We got a call from a woman saying she was getting beat up… that some guy was trying to kill her…? Know anything about that? *(SARAH nudges KAI, who moves away from her. He sees this and approaches SARAH.)* You… what's your name?

SARAH: *(With pride.)* Jean.

HARLEY: *(To POLICEMAN.)* Excuse me. Do you know where you are?

POLICEMAN: *(Whirling around.)* And who are you?

HARLEY: Harley Dolan. I'm the owner.

POLICEMAN: The owner of what?

HARLEY: The gym. This is a Boxing Girls Gym. *(She waits for him to get it.)*

POLICEMAN: "Boxing girls…?" *(HARLEY smiles and nods.)* Oh…. oh, boxing girls! Well, why didn't you say so…? *(Nodding.)*

HARLEY: You've heard of us?

POLICEMAN: Oh, yeah, the guys down at the station come over here all the time after their shifts. You know… work off a little steam…

HARLEY: Maybe you'd like a tour…?

SARAH: Wait… what about— *(Just then a boxing girl runs in. This is CONNIE. She's in her 20's, and her face is badly flushed and swollen.)*

CONNIE: Help…! Oh, my god. Thank god you're here… Help me! *(She clutches the POLICEMAN's arm, and begins sobbing hysterically.)*

POLICEMAN: *(Uncomfortable, he turns to HARLEY.)* I thought you said this was… what you call it…?

HARLEY: *(Smiling indulgently.)* Boxing Girls. It is. We're a legitimate gym. I can show you our license.

CONNIE: *(Focused on the POLICEMAN.)* He said he was going to kill me… He just kept hitting me—

POLICEMAN: *(Confused and suspicious.)* This don't look legitimate to me…

HARLEY: Just let me deal with it… *(She crosses to CONNIE and gently pulls her off the POLICEMAN's arm. She speaks slowly and directly to her, as if to a child.)* Connie, where is your client?

CONNIE: *(Confused.)* Whaaa..?

HARLEY: *(Reaching up to hold her face. CONNIE flinches with pain and a trauma response.)* Your client. The man who was sparring with you… I need you to tell me. Where is he?

CONNIE: *(Confused.)* "Sparring…?"

HARLEY: Connie, we need to know where he is.

CONNIE: I don't know.

HARLEY: Was he still in the gym, when you left?

CONNIE: Yes.

HARLEY: *(Turning to MARISA.)* Marisa!

MARISA: *(Jumping.)* What?

HARLEY: Marisa, I need you to go Gym 4, immediately.

MARISA: But—

HARLEY: Gym 4. And tell the client that you are tagging in for Connie… *(MARISA gets up.)* … and that we apologize for the interruption of service.

CONNIE: *(Grabbing MARISA.)* No! He's going to kill you! *(To the POLICEMAN.)* You don't understand! He's going to kill her!

HARLEY: *(Pulling CONNIE off MARISA, HARLEY stands between her and MARISA.)* Connie, let go. *(To MARISA.)* Did you hear me? *(HARLEY checks her watch.)* And I'll pay you the full fee, even though it's only half a round. Go! *(MARISA hesitates.)* GO! *(MARISA exits.)*

CONNIE: *(Struggling to get away from HARLEY in order to stop her.)* No! Marisa…!

HARLEY: *(Grabbing her again.)* Connie, *stop it!*

CONNIE: *(Turning in anguish to the POLICEMAN.)* He had his hands around my neck… Look…

HARLEY: *(To the POLICEMAN.)* That's not possible. We make all our clients wear protection.

POLICEMAN: Now, when you say "protection...?"

HARLEY: *(Exasperated.)* Gloves. Boxing gloves. We don't want anyone to get hurt. He couldn't have put his fingers around her neck, because of the gloves.

CONNIE: He took them off.

HARLEY: Now, why would he do that? He knows that's not allowed.

CONNIE: He said he wanted to feel it. *(Pointing again to her neck.)* See...? He had his fingers around my neck and he kept squeezing tighter and tighter... and I told him to stop, that I couldn't breath, and he laughed said that was the point—

HARLEY: *(Cutting in.)* Connie, did you hurt him?

CONNIE: What?

HARLEY: When you thought he had his hands around your neck, did you kick him... or claw him...?

CONNIE: I tried to pull his fingers away—

HARLEY: You didn't attack him in any way? *(A long silence. CONNIE is finally understanding.)*

CONNIE: No.

HARLEY: Good. *(She turns to the officer and shrugs.)* Nothing to report.

POLICEMAN: *(Suspicious, to CONNIE.)* If you didn't attack him, then how did you manage to call us and get away?

CONNIE: He was out of breath from punching me—

HARLEY: Connie, "sparring." You were his *legal* sparring partner.

CONNIE: *(A beat.)* ... and his face was all red, and he started to take off his gloves, so then I knew he was going to do something worse than punching... so while he was doing that, I was able to crawl under the ropes and get my phone, but while I was doing that, he got them off, and he came up behind me and grabbed me by the neck... *(Pointing again to the bruises.)* See...?

HARLEY: What did you do?

CONNIE: I pretended to pass out, and he dropped me to the floor, so I ran to the other side of the ring... So, now he was between me and the door, so we just stood there, because he knew if he came after me, I'd make it to the door before he did. So we were like that for a long time, and then I pretended like I was starting to faint, so then he came after me, but I ran around the other side of the ring and got to the door, and then I locked it.

HARLEY: *(Shocked.)* You *locked* it? *(CONNIE just stares at her.)* You *locked* the client in the gym? *(She shakes her head and turns to the POLICEMAN.)* Well, I suppose he has a claim for unlawful restraint if he wants to make it, but since Marisa hasn't come back, I think the most likely scenario is that he is finishing his round with her. But if you need to go talk to him— *(Just then the POLICEMAN's beeper goes off. He takes the call.)*

POLICEMAN: Yeah... *(Pause.)* Yeah... (Pause.) Where? *(Pause.)* Okay. *(Pause.)* Yeah. *(Pause.)* No... false alarm. I'm on my way. *(Hanging up, he turns to HARLEY.)* I got another call. I'll take a raincheck on that tour.

14

HARLEY: Okay. *(He turns to go.)* Oh! Here's a card. Just call any time and I can set up an appointment.

POLICEMAN: *(He takes it and looks at it.)* You got some more of these?

HARLEY: Sure… a whole stack. *(Handing them to him.)*

POLICEMAN: I'll pass 'em out at the station. *(Putting them in his pocket.)* Okay then… *(Turning somewhat awkwardly to CONNIE.)* Take care… *(He exits.)*

SARAH: Wait! What—

KAI: Hey… *(Holding SARAH's arm.)* Remember why we're here… Jean.

SARAH: But this woman almost got killed!

KAI: And Harley is dealing with it. Let the woman do her job. And you do yours. *(Still holding SARAH's arm.)*

HARLEY: Connie… *(CONNIE has slumped into one of the chairs, holding her head. HARLEY sits next to her)* Connie, look…

CONNIE: I guess I'll go home…

HARLEY: You don't need to do that. *(CONNIE shakes her head.)* Hang on… *(HARLEY crosses behind the counter and comes back with a jar of pills and a bottle of water.)* Here… Take these… *(CONNIE holds out her hand. HARELY counts out a specific number and opens the water bottle for CONNIE.)* Look, it's the end of the month, right? *(CONNIE takes the pills.)* Okay, rent's next week… right? *(CONNIE nods.)* And you've got a kid… a little girl…? *(CONNIE nods again.)* So, it's not

15

just you… *(She waits for CONNIE to nod. A long wait.)* You don't want to lose your kid, do you? *I* don't want to see that happen. *(Silence.)* Connie, honey—You've got to get your priorities straight… right? If you go home now, I can't pay you for today. I had to give the whole fee to Marisa to cover for you, remember? *(CONNIE's head falls down in her hands again.)* No, but listen… Here's what I can do. Elaine has a client tonight, and he's out-of-shape, not much of a boxer. Easy sparring. I'll see if she'll trade off with you, and you can give her one of your clients later. That way you can get your rent money. *(An arm around CONNIE.)* Honey, you have to get your head back in the game. *(Pause.)* Tell you what… take some time out… Go to the Makeup Room and fix your face. That always makes a girl feel better… Hey, try out the new massage chair I bought for you girls… Maybe take a little nap. Elaine's client won't be here until after six. By then, you'll be all fresh and ready to go again. How's that? *(Silence.)* That's the best we can do. *(CONNIE nods.)* More pills? *(CONNIE shakes her head.)* Atta girl. You got this. *(She exits.)*

SARAH: That's it? *(HARLEY, who has gone to put the pills back behind the counter, turns.)* That's it? That's all you're going to do?

HARLEY: What would you suggest?

SARAH: *(Extremely upset.)* She's just had the shit beat out of her and escaped an attempted murder… and he's got another victim in there, and you just let the police walk of here—

KAI: Jean—

SARAH: "Sarah." My name is "Sarah." And her name is "Kai," and we're doing a story for a magazine.

HARLEY: *What* magazine?

16

SARAH: It doesn't matter—

HARLEY: *(To KAI.)* WHAT magazine?

KAI: *Gentlemen.*

HARLEY: *(Relieved.)* Oh, yeah. They're okay.

SARAH: If you're not going to do anything, I will—

HARLEY: What? What are you going to do, tough girl? Pay her rent for her? Get her a job at Burger King, so she can dump her toddler in daycare for forty hours a week and still not afford groceries? She makes good money here. And that's her choice. She makes enough money where she only has to work a few hours a day. She can spend the rest of her time with her kid. Yeah, some days are harder than others, and this was one of them. Part of what she signed on for.

SARAH: Shut up! Shut up! This is bullshit, and you know it!

HARLEY: I know lot of women have it worse, every day, and they don't get paid at all. *(A beat.)* I used to be a boxing girl. I know what it's like. That's why I bought me a franchise. Do things a little different. The makeup room, the massage chair. I give 'em the pills so they don't get hooked… My girls *trust* me.

SARAH: It's criminal assault! Did you see her face? Just because someone pays to hit her, doesn't mean she's not going to feel it, not going to bruise, not going to have a black eye, not going to have her jaw dislocated!

HARLEY: Boxing. It can be a rough sport—

SARAH: *(Screaming.)* It's not a sport! It's *not a sport*! Only one person does the punching. That's not boxing!

HARLEY: Then I suppose you think prostitution isn't sex either…?

SARAH: *(Thrown.)* What?

HARLEY: *(Shaking her head, she turns to KAI.)* You and your friend, out.

SARAH: I'm taking that woman! She needs to go to the ER… and then to the police.

HARLEY: She doesn't want to go.

SARAH: I don't care. She's not staying here.

HARLEY: Lay a finger on her and it's assault. *(She picks up the phone and begins to dial.)* "Nine…one…" *(Looking up.)* And this is trespass right now. Both of you. I'm going to count to five and if you're not gone, I'm hitting that last digit. Your choice… *(Pause.)* One… Two…

KAI: Sarah, we gotta go..,

HARLEY: Three…

KAI: Come on!

HARLEY: Four…

KAI: We're going … We're going! *(She grabs SARAH. SARAH turns and shoves her. KAI grabs her again. SARAH shoves again.)*

SARAH: Don't do that again.

KAI: Come on! *(This time, when she grabs SARAH, SARAH throws a punch. KAI staggers back. HARLEY completes the call. She pulls out a gun from behind the counter and holds it on SARAH. SARAH freezes.)*

HARLEY: Got an assault-and-battery going on. Boxing Girls' Gym, 874 Franklin Boulevard… Nope… nobody hurt. I got a gun on the assailant… *(KAI slips out the door. HARLEY hangs up the phone.)* You know, it can be tough to get work when you've got a criminal record… *(SARAH glares.)* Tell you what… look us up, and I'll give you a job. You won't have to intern.

End of Play

The Intimacy Coach

Summary

Lights come up on the interior of a room in a present-day brothel. Jewell, wearing a robe, is preparing for an assignation with a client. There is a knock on the door and Stan enters. He is late because of traffic and annoyed that Jewell will not extend the appointment. As his pants come off, Jewell notes that he needs to leave his belt at the reception desk downstairs. He is annoyed to be losing any more time. On his return, he undresses for a second time, but there is another knock on the door and Jewell goes to see who it is. It's Marsha, who claims she is an intimacy coordinator that the brothel has hired to ensure the safety of clients and staff. Stan, with growing frustration, puts on his pants again, as Jewell allows Marsha to enter.

As Marsha starts to explain that intimacy coordinators are hired in theatre and film to protect the performers, Stan interrupts, protesting that the sex is not going to involve scenarios or anything dangerous—in other words, no theatre. Marsha points out that Stan will be having a sexual experience, but that Jewell will not. She will actually be performing the role of a woman who is desirous of his attention, and this will require the mutual signing of a consent form. Stan is unable to grasp this concept, and, exasperated, Jewell orders him to leave, holding out his pants.

After Stan's departure, Jewell confronts Marsha, accusing her of being an evangelist or a man-hater. Marsha reveals she is a former prostitute, and Jewell calls her out on her "sex policing," insisting that consent is already institutionalized in the brothel.

Marsha counters with shocking percentages of prostitutes with sexual abuse histories and percentages who express a desire to leave, but who are trapped by lack of resources. She points out that prostitution will never lose its stigma until these victims and captives are gone and that, when they are gone, women like Jewell will be able to name their prices.

Jewell, who has put up a good front, is actually intrigued and asks Marsha to make an appointment with her in a week. Marsha goes to shake hands with Jewell, and Jewell counters with a reference to the language in the consent form: "Skin, muscle, or bone?" Marsha responds with "Bone—Touch Level Three" and they shake.

2 women, 1 man
Single set
20 minutes

Cast of Characters

STAN: A male, thirties or forties, any race, any ethnicity.

JEWELL: A woman in her thirties, any race, any ethnicity.

MARSHA: A woman in her thirties, any race, any ethnicity.

Scene

Private room in a brothel.

Time

The present.

The Intimacy Coordinator

Lights come up in a private room in a brothel. There is a large bed, two chairs, and a small round table with an ashtray. JEWELL, a woman in her 20's, sits at the table putting on makeup, using a small compact. She is wearing a skimpy slip with a shiny robe, stockings, and a garter belt. Just finishing, she peers at her watch, and then rises and begins to pace. She stops at the door, opens it and looks up and down the hall. She turns back to check her makeup again, and there is a knock on the door. She crosses to the door and opens it. STAN is in the doorway. A male in his thirties or forties, he wears casual clothing. He is distracted and harried.

STAN: Sorry I'm late. Traffic jam.

JEWELL: *(Shrugging.)* It's your time, honey.

STAN: *(Surprised.)* Hey, come on… There was a traffic jam. It's not my fault. *(Hurriedly, he begins to take off his shirt*

JEWELL: You think it's mine?

STAN: No, but, come on… I'm paying three hundred dollars an hour here… Cut me some slack… *(The shirt is off.)*

JEWELL: That's right—three hundred dollars an hour, and I'm not giving it away just because you didn't bother to get here on time.

STAN: It was the traffic!

JEWELL: *(Shaking her head.)* Not my problem.

STAN: Oh, come on…!

25

JEWELL: Tik-tok.

STAN: Okay, okay. *(Annoyed, he begins to tug on his belt.)*

JEWELL: Nice to meet you, too.

STAN: I'm Stan. *(Still yanking at his belt, not looking up.)*

JEWELL: I'm Jewell. *(Seeing that he's not listening.)* But you can call me Jewell.

STAN: Yeah. Nice to meet you. *(He finally frees the belt and pulls down his pants. He turns to face her, annoyed.)* Jewell.

JEWELL: Belt?

STAN: What?

JEWELL: That's a belt. They're not allowed up here. You have to leave it at the front desk.

STAN: What?

JEWELL: House rules. Belts and ties. At the front desk.

STAN: Oh, for chrissake! *(He yanks his pants on again, grabs the belt and heads out the door. JEWELL paces again, checking her makeup.. STAN returns. He's been running.)* Okay… let's get going. *(He pulls down his pants. There's a knock on the door.)* Who the hell's that?

JEWELL: I don't know. *(In the direction of the door.)* Busy! *(The knock comes again. And JEWELL yells again.)* I said I'm busy! Talk to the receptionist! *(More knocking. JEWELL turns and looks at STAN. Panicked, he yanks his pants on again. More knocking.)*

JEWELL: All right, all right! *(She whips open the door. MARSHA is standing there. She is a woman in her 30's, wearing a business suit and carrying a briefcase.)* What do you want?

MARSHA: Are you Jewell?

JEWELL: Who's asking?

MARSHA: Marsha Lyon. *(She holds out a business card.)*

JEWELL: *(Closing the door.)* I'm busy.

MARSHA: *(Foot in the door.)* I need to speak with you.

JEWELL: Schedule downstairs.

MARSHA: I did.

JEWELL: I don't think so. This appointment's been on the books for two weeks. *(A beat. She spells it out.) I'm with a client.*

MARSHA: Yes. I know, and I need to speak with both of you, which is why I am here now. *(She offers the business card again, and this time JEWELL takes it and reads it. Looking up, she sees that STAN is staring at her. She passes him the card and continues to look at MARSHA.)*

STAN: *(Reading.)* What the hell...? What's an "intimacy coordinator?"

JEWELL: Don't look at me.

STAN: *(To MARSHA.)* Are you a sex therapist?

MARSHA: Not exactly.

STAN: Yeah, well, we don't need anything like that... Jewell here is a professional. She doesn't need any help... And we're kind of in a hurry here, so if you don't mind...

JEWELL: *(Appraising MARSHA with a mocking smile.)* "Intimacy coordinator..."

MARSHA: *(Ignoring the implication of JEWELL's smile.)* It's a protection for you, for the client *(Indicating STAN)*, and for your establishment. That's why your employer has retained my services and sent me here.

STAN: *(Nervous and defensive.)* Look, I'm not into any of the kinky shit. No whips, no cutting, no bondage, no gags, no choking... Nobody's going to get hurt here. We're just going to have some good, old-fashioned, all-American sex.

MARSHA: I am still going to need signatures from both of you on these forms. *(Opening the brief case.)*

STAN: *(Quickly.)* Oh, I'm not signing anything.

MARSHA: *(Sorting through the forms.)* Originally intimacy coordinators were hired by theatres and film studios to ensure the safety and comfort of the actors who were being required to perform sexual or romantic scenes—

STAN: *(Interrupting.)* No, see... Nobody's acting out any scenarios. Nobody's going to be filming anything. Just plain old sex. Me and her. That's all.

MARSHA: *(Still sorting her forms.)* These consent forms are to assure that all the choreography is agreed on—

STAN: *(Cutting her off, increasingly annoyed.)* No! No! There's not going to be any show! There's no lap dance, no

28

strippers… Nothing to choreograph. *(He turns to JEWELL for backup. A beat.)*

JEWELL: *(To MARSHA)* Let me see these fucking forms… *(MARSHA hands them to her, and she looks them over.)* This is some kind of joke, right? *(MARSHA smiles.)* "Check-in?" Seriously…? *Check-in?* "Personal boundaries…?" Who the hell sent you?

STAN: *(Talking to himself.)* You know what…? I don't care. What the hell… *(He takes off his pants for the third time.)*

JEWELL: *(Looking up.)* Hey, Stan, you planning on touching my "upper chest region" today?

STAN: *(Confused and disoriented—and pantless.)* What?

JEWELL: Or my "back pelvis area?"

STAN: *(Lost.)* "Back pelvis" what?

JEWELL: Boobs and butt. Are you going to touch my boobs or my butt today? Because this lady seems to think that's her business.

STAN: I don't know what—

JEWELL: *(Cutting him off.)* And if you are, she needs to know if you're going to be touching just the skin, or the muscle, or if you're going to go all the way to the bone. *(Consulting the form.)* "Touch Level One, Two or Three…"

MARSHA: *(Unruffled, she smiles.)* It's called "consent."

JEWELL: She wants to know if you will be "opening and closing the distance between our pelvises."

STAN: *(Despairing.)* Opening the what…? I don't… This… What…?

MARSHA *(To JEWELL.)* The language is intentionally non-sexual to keep the interaction professional and non-triggering.

STAN: *(Whining.)* I just want to have sex. I paid three hundred dollars, and I'm already out fifty dollars for a traffic jam that wasn't my fault, because I left in plenty of time. In fact, I was going to be early. *(To JEWELL.) I was going to be early! (Back to MARSHA.)* But still… out fifty dollars, and then nobody told me about the belts and ties, and she waits until I've got my pants off to tell me, so that's five minutes there… that's twenty-five dollars… So now I'm out seventy-five, and now you're here and it's another fifty dollars I'm paying for, and I don't even know *what* this is about…

MARSHA: *(Speaking slowly.)* It's about sex. You said you were going to have sex.

STAN: Yes.

MARSHA: But what about Jewell?

STAN: What *about* Jewell?

MARSHA: Is she going to have be having sex?

STAN: Well, yeah. Takes two to tango.

MARSHA: But will she actually "be having sex?"

STAN: *(Measuring his words.)* Yes. She will be having sex. With me. *(There's a long and tense silence.)*

MARSHA: I'm confused. Is Jewell paying you?

STAN: *(Confused.)* No…

MARSHA: Is she dating you?

STAN: No…

MARSHA: *(Turning to JEWELL.)* Jewell, would you be allowing your client to have sex with you if he wasn't paying you?

JEWELL: *(Having figured out MARSHA's game, JEWELL nods and smiles.)* Well, "Marsha," I guess we will never know, since he *is* paying me.

STAN: *(Despondently.)* Three hundred dollars.

MARSHA: Well, "Jewell," I think we *can* know, because your client would be a fool to pay for something he could otherwise get for free—

JEWELL: *(She's had enough.)* Okay. So this has been a barrel of laughs, but now it's time for you to go. *(She gathers up the papers and crosses to the door.)*

MARSHA: As soon as you finalize the consent forms.

JEWELL: *(Smiling, she hands MARSHA the papers.)* You know I'm not going to do that.

MARSHA: Why not?

JEWELL: Because that's not part of my job.

MARSHA: *(Surprised.)* Consent is not part of your job…?

JEWELL: I didn't say that.

MARSHA: Oh, I think you just did. *(STAN has crossed to the chair, where he slumps down, looking at his watch. MARSHA begins to pace like an attorney lecturing the jury.)* If you are not physically attracted to Stan, or "turned on by him," and your motive for allowing him physical access to your body is money, then the service you are actually providing is a *performance*. You are being paid to enact the role of someone sexually attracted to or "turned on" by Stan—someone who desires him physically. And precisely because it *is* a performance—a performance for which there is a monetary compensation—every step of that performance must be carefully choreographed to ensure that the consent is both mutual and ongoing throughout the interaction. Otherwise, of course, it can be construed, in the eyes of the law, as harassment and especially as assault. *(There is a long silence.)*

JEWELL: *(Nodding slowly, she looks at STAN and then at MARSHA and then back to STAN. She makes a sudden decision.)* Stan, I think you better go.

STAN: *(Lifting his head.)* What?

JEWELL: *(Not taking her eyes off MARSHA, JEWELL speaks with increasing certainty.)* You need to go, Stan. They can reschedule you at the front desk. *(She holds out his pants.)*

STAN: *(Staring at the pants.)* I… I don't understand.

JEWELL: *(Eyes on MARSHA.)* And you don't have to. That's part of what you pay for. But this appointment is over.

STAN: But—

JEWELL: *(Still extending the pants.)* Now! Do *not* make me ring for the bouncer.

STAN: *(Standing up and grabbing the pants.)* Okay… okay… You don't have to yell. *(He tries to pull them on but trips in his haste, and ends by grabbing his shirt and waddling out the door, pants around his ankles.)* I'm going… I'm going... *(STAN exits and JEWELL closes the door behind him. She turns

32

to confront MARSHA. MARSHA smiles at her. There is a long moment.)

JEWELL: So who's paying you?

MARSHA: Your boss.

JEWELL: No, he's not. Who put you up to this?

MARSHA: Up to what?

JEWELL: "Intimacy coordinator?" That was quite the act. What else can you do?

MARSHA: Isn't that enough? I made a man disappear, didn't I?

JEWELL: No, you didn't. *I* got rid of him. Don't flatter yourself. If I wanted him here, you would be gone. He showed up late, bitching about getting overtime. *(She takes out a cigarette.)* I don't work with clients who are whiny little bitches. *(She lights the cigarette.)*

MARSHA: Could you please put that out. *(A beat.)* I'm allergic. *(JEWELL looks at her, takes a drag and exhales, considers the request, and slowly puts it out. MARSHA watches her.)* How would you like to work with me…?

JEWELL: *(Shaking her head in disbelief.)* So who put you up to this? *(MARSHA smiles.)* Right-wing religious organization? Left-wing radical feminists? *(A beat.)* Who paid you to interrupt my business today?

MARSHA: *(A beat.)* What if I told you that I work for myself?

JEWELL: Same question: Right-wing religious nut or left-wing men-hater?

MARSHA: Former prostitute.

JEWELL: *(Nodding.)* So a little bit of both. *(Rising, she walks around MARSHA.)* Let me guess… Your father…? No? Uncle…? Grandfather…? Brother? *(MARSHA smiles slightly.)* Ah. Brother. *(Musing.)* Your brother raped you when you were a child and nobody believed you, and so you started acting out, because as long as people are going to believe you're a bad girl, you might as well be one…? *(JEWELL pauses, but MARSHA doesn't say anything.)* So… *then* you started acting out at school… had some trouble with alcohol or drugs...? *(Looking at MARSHA.)* Both…? Interesting… And then you got a reputation for being a slut or a psycho… or both. *(MARSHA looks at her.)* And *then* some older man—your sympathetic art teacher?—came along and "exploited your vulnerability," and you believed he loved you, and, of course, you were "in love" with him… the first in a long line of daddies… And eventually, one of them would turn out to be a pimp, but of course, you wouldn't catch on until it was too late. And then fast-forward to that magical day when some emergency room doctor, or some public health nurse, or some battered-women's-shelter counselor, or some flyer glued on the door of a toilet stall at the YWCA, or some book, or some movie, or some tweet opened your eyes to the fact that you are a victim, and—in fact—your whole life you have never been anything but a victim, and that nothing is your fault, and that everything you have ever done was just in an effort to survive. And so now, you are on a mission to open the eyes of your former sisters who are still toiling away in ignorance and shame, victims of the patriarchy and betrayers of their sex. *(A beat.)* Did I miss anything? *(There is a long silence.)*

MARSHA: Some.

JEWELL: Well, I think you're missing some, too. *(A beat.)* Not everyone who works this job is a victim.

MARSHA: I used to say that.

JEWELL: Yeah, well some of us say that and we actually mean it. Some of us have looked hard at our options, and we actually made an informed decision that this job is a good fit for us. We like what we do. Our clients like what we do. Our bosses like what we do. And you know what? We're damn good at it. We earn a lot of money for making everybody happy. It's a win-win. And we like that. You know, race car driving is dangerous, too. *(MARSHA nods.)*

MARSHA: Okay, but you couldn't fill out the consent forms.

JEWELL: Didn't need to. I understand what I've agreed to.

MARSHA: So do I. You consent to waive consent.

JEWELL: No, we negotiate.

MARSHA: Maybe on the basics… anal, oral, BDSM… but what about everything else…? *How* he touches you, *when* he touches you, *what* he gets to say to you, *if* he kisses you, *where* he—

JEWELL: For three hundred dollars an hour, I really don't give a crap. *(A beat.)* You picked the wrong woman to try to convert.

MARSHA: I couldn't have picked a better one.

JEWELL: No, see, I don't have a problem with prostitution.

MARSHA: Yes, but much of the rest of the world does—

JEWELL: And I don't give a shit what they think.

MARSHA: If you like your job as much as you say you do, then you better "give a shit."

35

JEWELL: Why?

MARSHA: Because there are a lot of people who are out there working twenty-four/seven to abolish prostitution, and they're not all right-wing, or men-hating nut jobs. I mean, just look at the Nordic model—*(JEWELL shakes her head in disgust.)* Yeah, I know… It criminalizes the buyers and decriminalizes the prostitute. How crazy is that?

JEWELL: Like we're all victiims…

MARSHA: But it's already the law in Sweden, Norway, Iceland, Ireland, Canada, France, Israel—

JEWELL: *(Shaking her head.)* Sex police.

MARSHA: It's women like you who are the only ones who can turn this victim narrative around.

JEWELL: How?

MARSHA: *(Holding up the forms.)* The consent forms.

JEWELL: They're a joke.

MARSHA: Now, hang on. Ask yourself, "How can I get the world to understand that it's not only legitimate work, but an empowering career choice for women… a path to self-esteem, financial independence, and public recognition for providing a service to humanity?"

JEWELL: "Upper chest region…?"

MARSHA: *(There's a long silence.)* So the average age of girls entering prostitution is twelve to fourteen years old…

JEWELL: No it's not—

MARSHA: Yes. It is.

JEWELL: Who says?

MARSHA: About every study ever done. Look… this is going to be a fight, and you're not going to win it by ignoring the facts. People tried to do that in Sweden, Norway, Iceland—and that's how they lost.

JEWELL: Okay, okay… I'm listening.

MARSHA: Well, these statistics make it pretty easy for people to believe that prostitutes are victims. *(JEWEL starts to say something.)* No, wait… so…

JEWELL: *(Distrustful.)* So…?

MARSHA: Get them out. *(A beat.)* Get the victims out. People are never going to believe that anyone prostituted as a child is anything but a victim. You can see that, right? *(Long, long silence.)*

JEWELL: *(Suddenly pushing back from the table.)* So that's the pitch, isn't it? You thought you had me going, didn't you? *(Deliberately, she lights a cigarette.)*

MARSHA: *(Shrugging.)* Do a search.

JEWELL: *(Blowing smoke in MARSHA's direction.)* What? You mean the statistics? So what? Nobody cares about those girls. You should know that. You were one of them.

MARSHA: Sweden, Norway, Iceland, Ireland—

JEWELL: *(Cutting her off.)* Okay, okay! But you. Let's talk about you. You're not really interested in "polishing the

37

image," are you? You want to shut the whole thing down. *(Silence.)* Yeah. I thought so. You quitters are all the same.

MARSHA: Okay. Yeah. But… forty-two million prostituted women and girls in the world…? The odds are not really in my favor, are they?

JEWELL: *(Exhaling.)* Nope.

MARSHA: But you and I actually have a lot of common ground.

JEWELL: I don't think so.

MARSHA: Well, give me a chance. *(A beat.)* So here's the "pitch," as you call it—why you should work with me as an intimacy coordinator. *(Silence. MARSHA picks up the consent form.)* The consent form is actually about re-education, about consciousness-raising. These women who were brought in as children never learned what consent looks like, and, even if they did, they never learned they had a right to it. It was knowledge that was either withheld or distorted in order to coerce them. So… here… look… *(She crosses over to JEWELL and points to a section of one of the forms.)* …levels of touch, specific naming of parts of anatomy and sequence of actions, duration of touch… It's a back-to-basics primer on what it means to have control over physical intimacy. Think of it like remedial learning. Now, maybe I'm wrong, but I think it's reasonable to assume that many or even most of these women and girls who were prostituted as children will realize that they never chose this life and that, possibly, they are not choosing it now…

JEWELL: I don't think that's a reasonable assumption at all.

MARSHA: Why not?

JEWELL: *(Short laugh.)* Because of the money.

MARSHA: Well, that's actually the second public relations issue…

JEWELL: The money?

MARSHA: Around ninety percent of prostitutes report wanting to get out of prostitution, but say they lack the resources to leave.

JEWELL: That's total bullshit.

MARSHA: No, it's not. That's real… study after study, country after country, demographic after demographic.

JEWELL: Ninety percent… I don't believe it.

MARSHA: Well, okay, but let's just suppose for a moment that it's true. That could potentially put you in a pretty powerful position. *(She pauses. JEWELL leans in.)* What if everyone who wanted out could suddenly actually get out… Ninety percent. Demand would far exceed supply, and women like you could set your own prices… like free agent professional athletes.

JEWELL: Yeah, but that's never going to happen. Who's going to get the money for all these millions of women to leave?

MARSHA: Intimacy coordinators.

JEWELL: Yeah, right.

MARSHA: Hang on. The consent form actually documents in detail and with clinical precision the agreements between prostitutes and their clients. It has both signatures and it's a legal agreement… *(A beat.)* Look—you and I both know that what goes on in these rooms would constitute creation of a hostile work environment, sexual harassment, and rape if it were happening in any other place of employment.

JEWELL: And race car driving would be reckless endangerment—What's your point?

MARSHA: My point is, statistically about three quarters of prostitutes are raped at least once a year. Not you, of course… but that's the statistic. As an intimacy coordinator, you will be in a position to support these women—the ninety percent who want out—by providing them with the documentation they need to take the brothel owners to court and, of course, the settlement money would provide the resources needed to leave.

JEWELL: Who pays you? Who would pay me?

MARSHA: Who pays for any revolution? We get our money from many sources, but I can't tell you who, because it's too dangerous.

JEWELL: Dangerous?

MARSHA: Undergound. It's like trying to form a union. The owners don't want to see the workers take control. As you said yourself, they don't give a shit about these girls who come in without consent, and they don't give a shit about the women who feel trapped. The more the merrier. And they certainly don't want to see women like yourself acting as free agents. *(MARSHA retrieves the forms.)* There is nothing more dangerous than a consent form. *(She puts them in her briefcase, snaps it shut, and turns toward JEWELL.)* You have my card. *(She starts to exit.)*

JEWELL: *(Callling out.)* Make an appointment…! *(MARSHA stops and turns.)* On your way out. Make an appointment with me for next week.

MARSHA: So, we have a deal? *(She extends her hand. JEWELL looks at it.)*

JEWELL: Skin, muscle, or bone?

40

MARSHA: *(Smiling warmly.)* Touch Level Three… Bone. *(A beat. JEWELL extends her hand and the women shake. They continue to clasp hands as the lights fade.)*

Blackout

End of Play

www.ingramcontent.com/pod-product-compliance
Lightning Source LLC
Chambersburg PA
CBHW070341290526
45791CB00003B/1423